How Did We
Find Out About
Pluto?

The "HOW DID WE FIND OUT . . . ?" series
by Isaac Asimov

HOW DID WE FIND OUT—

How Did We Find Out About Pluto?

Isaac Asimov

Illustrated by Erika Kors

Walker and Company
New York

First published in the United States of America in 1991
by Walker Publishing Company, Inc.

Published simultaneously in Canada by Thomas Allen & Son
Canada, Limited, Markham, Ontario

Library of Congress Cataloging-in-Publication Data

Asimov, Isaac, date.
    How did we find out about Pluto? / Isaac Asimov; illustrated by
Erika Kors.
      p. cm.
    Summary: Describes the history of Pluto's discovery and what is
known and unknown about the planet today.
    ISBN 0-8027-6991-8.—ISBN 0-8027-6992-6 (reinf.)
    1. Pluto (Planet)—Juvenile literature.   [1. Pluto (Planet)]
I. Kors, Erika W., ill. II. Title.
QB701.A84   1990
523.4'82—dc20   90-42542
                                                  CIP
                                                  AC

Printed in the United States of America

10 9 8 7 6 5 4 3 2 1

Dedicated to
my nephew,
Larry Repanes, and his brand-new daughter

Contents

1
Uranus and Neptune

THE PLANET URANUS is the seventh planet out from
the Sun. It is about 1,784 million miles from the Sun,
or about nineteen times as far from the Sun as the
Earth is. It takes 84 years for Uranus to make one
journey around the Sun.

Uranus was discovered in 1781 and, after that, was
very closely studied by astronomers. They expected it
to move about the Sun in a certain way, according to
the law of gravitation first worked out by the English
scientist Isaac Newton (1642–1727) in 1687. According
to this law, the Sun ought to exert a strong gravitational pull on Uranus, a pull governed by the sizes of
the Sun and Uranus and the distance between them.

Jupiter and Saturn, which are the largest planets and also the two closest to Uranus, ought to exert small gravitational pulls of their own.

If the pulls of the Sun, Jupiter, and Saturn were all taken into account, Uranus ought to move around the Sun in a certain elliptical orbit. In moving so it would, as seen from Earth, move among the stars in a certain path from night to night and astronomers should be able to tell exactly where it would be every night.

The trouble was that this turned out not to be so. With time, Uranus slowly moved out of the calculated position. The error wouldn't seem much to ordinary people, but to astronomers it was a horrifying situation. It might have meant that Newton's law of gravitation was wrong. And if that were the case astronomy might find itself in a very confused situation.

Astronomers decided that the trouble was that they weren't considering all the different gravitational pulls. Suppose there were another planet beyond Uranus that had not yet been discovered. It would exert a small pull on Uranus that in turn might cause those errors in its position that were troubling astronomers.

Two astronomers tried to calculate where the unknown planet might be if it were to produce the errors that were being noted in Uranus's motion. One was a British astronomer, John Couch Adams (1819–1892), and the other was a French astronomer, Urbain Jean Joseph Leverrier (luh-veh-RYAY, 1811–1877). Each one worked on the problem without knowing that the other was also working on it.

The problem was very difficult, but both Adams

John Couch Adams and Urbain Jean Joseph Leverrier played
a key role in the discovery of Neptune, independently
predicting quite accurately the position in the sky where
Neptune would be found.

and Leverrier were excellent mathematicians. In 1845, Adams got an answer, and in 1846, Leverrier got an answer. Each ended with just about the same answer. The unknown planet would have to be located in a certain spot in the sky if it were to be responsible for the error in Uranus's motion.

It took a while to get astronomers with good telescopes to look for the planet in the spot that Adams and Leverrier had indicated. However, on September 23, 1846, two German astronomers, Johann Gottfried Galle (GAHL-uh, 1812–1910) and Heinrich Ludwig d'Arrest (dah-REH, 1822–1875), looked in the region of the predicted spot and within an hour found a planet.

Astronomers named this planet, which was the eighth planet out from the Sun, Neptune. The discovery was a mighty victory for the law of gravitation, for using that law, two astronomers had managed to work out where a new and undiscovered planet ought to be—and there it was.

Once Neptune's actual distance (about 2,792 million miles from the Sun or about thirty times our own distance from the Sun) was determined and its size and motions all worked out, its gravitational pull on Uranus could be calculated. And behold, Uranus's supposed error in motion was explained away.

Yet it was not an entirely happy ending, for Uranus's error of motion was not *completely* explained away. There was still a tiny error remaining.

Could there be still another planet even beyond Neptune? If so, this other planet, being still farther from Uranus than Neptune was, would have a weaker gravitational pull on Uranus. That weak pull might just account for the last little bit of error.

Of course, this additional unknown planet beyond Neptune would be closer to Neptune than to Uranus, and it ought to have a stronger effect on Neptune. Why bother with Uranus's tiny error? Just keep an eye on Neptune's motion.

However, it doesn't work that way. The more times a planet travels around the Sun, the more accurately astronomers can measure a tiny error in its motion. Uranus had been discovered in 1781, and by 1846, when astronomers were looking for Neptune, Uranus had made three-quarters of its circle around the Sun, and the errors were clear. By the year 1900 it had made one and two-fifths trips around the Sun, and by then even tiny errors in its motion had been measured.

Neptune, on the other hand, had been discovered in 1846, and it took 165 years to go around the Sun. By 1900 Neptune had gone only one-third the way around the Sun. For that reason it was safer to rely on the smaller errors in Uranus's motion, rather than on what might eventually turn out to be larger errors in Neptune's motion.

Still, very few astronomers thought it worthwhile to search for a new, more distant planet. There were several reasons for this.

First, there was the matter of brightness. All the planets that were known from ancient times are very bright and easy to see. These are Mercury, Venus, Mars, Jupiter, and Saturn. They are *first-magnitude* objects. Venus and Jupiter are particularly brilliant. In fact, there are few stars as bright, so the very bright planets stand out and are noticeable.

Dimmer stars have higher magnitudes—2, 3, 4, and so on. The higher the magnitude, the dimmer the star. The dimmest stars we can see with the unaided eye have a magnitude of about 6. The higher the magnitude, the more stars there are of that magnitude. Only about twenty stars are, like the planets, of magnitude 1. However, there are almost five thousand stars of magnitudes 5 and 6.

Uranus is twice as far away as Saturn and considerably smaller. The light it reflects is much weaker, therefore, and its magnitude is only 5.5. It can just barely be seen by the unaided eye and is surrounded by thousands of stars of the same brightness, so it is much harder to notice than the other planets.

Then, too, while ordinary stars maintain the same positions with respect to each other, night after night and year after year, the planets move against the background of the stars. This motion can be used to identify a planet and prove that it is not a star. However, the farther a planet is from the Sun, the more slowly it moves. Uranus moves so slowly that a careful astronomer is needed to note that it is moving. In other words, Uranus is so dim and moves so slowly that it's not surprising it was discovered only in 1781, when the other planets were discovered in ancient times.

Neptune is still farther away than Uranus, so it is even dimmer. Its magnitude is 7.8, so it can't be seen at all without a telescope. What's more, it moves even more slowly than Uranus and is surrounded by tens of

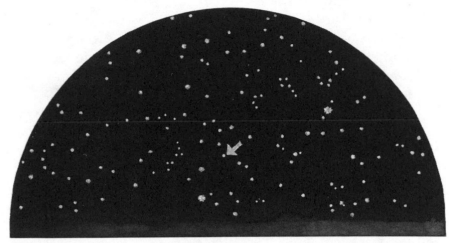

East   West

Neptune's position in the sky when it was discovered by two
German astronomers on the night of September 23, 1846.

thousands of stars of the same brightness. It is even
harder to find than Uranus, which is why it was not
discovered until 1846.

Neptune wouldn't have been discovered even then
if Adams and Leverrier had not worked out where it
ought to be by calculating its position from the error
in Uranus's motion.

If there were a planet beyond Neptune, it would be
still dimmer than Neptune, it would move even more
slowly, and it would be surrounded by hundreds of
thousands of stars of the same brightness. What's
more, the remaining errors in Uranus's motion were

so tiny that trying to get a hint by calculating where it ought to be was a task much more difficult than Adams and Leverrier had faced.

To be sure, astronomers could now take photographs of the stars, which Adams and Leverrier couldn't do in their time, and that simplified the task somewhat—but not enough. Most astronomers simply felt that a search for a planet beyond Neptune was just a waste of time, and so they made no effort in that direction.

2
Percival
Lowell

ONE PERSON DARED to be different. He was Percival Lowell (1855–1916). Lowell had been born to an aristocratic Boston family and had made a great deal of money in business. He was also a skilled mathematician. His hobby was astronomy, and he was particularly interested in the planet Mars.

In 1877, an Italian astronomer, Giovanni Virginio Schiaparelli (1835–1910), had studied Mars closely and made a map of the markings he could see on it. He thought the dark markings might represent water, and the light markings, land. He noticed that some of the dark markings were long and narrow, and he called them *canali*, which is Italian for "channel." A channel is any long, narrow body of water connecting two larger bodies. The English Channel between England and France is the best-known example on Earth of a body of water known by that name.

The word, however, was translated into English as *canals*. This was unfortunate, because a canal is an artificial waterway dug out by humans. As soon as English-speaking people heard that there were "canals" on Mars, they believed there were intelligent beings on Mars. They also thought that Mars, being smaller than the Earth and having only two-fifths its gravitational pull, was not able to hold water over long periods. For that reason, Mars was drying out, and the Martians must have dug the canals to conduct water from the planet's polar ice caps to the warmer regions near its equator, where they could grow food.

Lowell was very interested in the Martian canals, and he made up his mind to study them with great care. He used his fortune to establish a private observatory in Flagstaff, Arizona, where the altitude, the desert air, and the remoteness from city lights made the night sky particularly clear. The Lowell Observatory opened in 1894.

For fifteen years, Lowell studied Mars as carefully as he could, taking thousands of photographs. He was sure that he could make out the canals. In fact, he saw far more than Schiaparelli ever did, and he drew detailed pictures that eventually included over five hundred canals. These followed straight lines that crossed one another. At the crossings, the dark areas seemed to broaden, and Lowell called these *oases*.

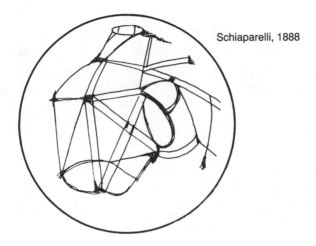

Schiaparelli, 1888

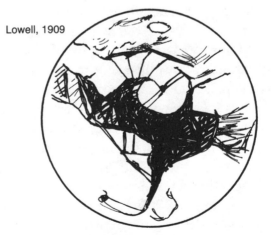

Lowell, 1909

Maps of Mars made by Giovanni Schiaparelli and Percival
Lowell, showing lines that Schiaparelli thought were channels
and that Lowell thought were canals.

The canals seemed to become double at times. There were changes with the Martian seasons.

Lowell lectured on the subject, wrote popular books, and was completely covinced that there was intelligent life on Mars. As a result, the British writer Herbert George (H. G.) Wells (1866–1946) wrote a book in 1898 called *The War of the Worlds* in which he described a Martian invasion of Earth. This made the notion of intelligent (and dangerous) life on Mars even more popular.

Few other astronomers managed to see the canals the way that Lowell did, but Lowell wasn't upset by that. He simply pointed out that he had better eyes, a better telescope, and a better observatory.

Yet, as it turned out, Lowell was wrong. We now know that there are no canals on Mars. We have sent unmanned spacecraft to Mars since the 1960s, and they have mapped the whole planet in detail. They found no canals and no signs of any intelligent life. Apparently, Lowell, trying to see things he could just barely make out, was fooled by optical illusions. Little patches of irregular dark markings seem to form straight lines when the eyes strain to see them.

Nevertheless, all this showed that Lowell was not afraid to take up difficult tasks and to deal with subjects that other astronomers avoided.

Beginning in 1902, Lowell became interested in the possible existence of a planet beyond Neptune. In 1905, he began a search for the planet, keeping that search a secret so that other astronomers wouldn't take up the task and perhaps beat him to the discov-

Percival Lowell viewing the heavens at his observatory
in Flagstaff, Arizona.

ery. In 1908, he began to call the unknown distant world Planet X.

Lowell's secrecy was of no use, however. Another aristocratic Boston astronomer, William Henry Pickering (1858–1938), was also interested in the possible existence of a planet beyond Neptune. Pickering had already made some discoveries about the outer planets. In 1898, for instance, he had detected a ninth satellite of Saturn, one that was farther from the planet than any of the others. He called it Phoebe.

Pickering used the tiny errors in Uranus's motion to venture an estimate of the location of a planet beyond Neptune (a planet which he called Planet O). He believed that the planet beyond Neptune would probably be about 4,800 million miles from the Sun, or about one and three-quarters times as far from the Sun as Neptune is. It would take 373 years to move once around the Sun, or two and one-quarter times as long as it takes Neptune to make its own circuit. Pickering also believed that the new planet would be about twice the mass of Earth. In addition, he believed that its magnitude would be between 11 and 13, which meant it would be surrounded by millions of stars of the same brightness.

Pickering announced his figures in 1908. When Lowell heard this, he was upset and decided to do some figuring of his own. His results predicted that the distant planet was about 4,400 million miles from the Sun, a little nearer than Pickering thought, and that it would go around the Sun in 327 years, again less than Pickering's figure. He also thought it would be about six or seven times the mass of the Earth, or almost half the size of Uranus or Neptune.

Pickering, however, did not follow up his figures by actually trying to find the planet in the sky. But Lowell was more determined.

He began what was an enormous task. He made photographs of sections of the sky under conditions that would pick up stars as dim as magnitude 13. Such a photograph might contain hundreds of thousands of stars. He would then take another photograph of the same part of the sky a few days later. All the dim stars on it would remain in place, but if one of the stars was actually a new planet, that "star" would have changed its position slightly.

Lowell would then search the two photographs with a magnifying glass, looking at each star and trying to see if he could detect a change. It was the kind of work that led to one disappointment after another, and by 1912, Lowell suffered a nervous collapse. He later recovered, however, and went right back to the search.

Lowell died of a stroke in 1916, and at the time of his death, he had still not found the planet. He was only 61 when he died, and his life may well have been shortened by his continuous searching.

Toward the end, however, he had found a better way of looking for the planet. This was through the use of a *blink comparator*. Carl Otto Lampland (1873–1951), then the assistant director of the Lowell Observatory, had urged Lowell to get this device, and finally he did. This is how it worked.

Two photographic plates were taken of a particular

sector of sky a few days apart. These two plates were placed in the blink comparator, which shone a light through one of the plates and projected it onto a screen. Then it shone a light through the other negative and projected it onto the same screen. The blink comparator switched from one negative to the other, back and forth, back and forth, very quickly. If the plates didn't fall on exactly the same part of the screen, the stars would appear first in one place, then in the other, shuttling back and forth rapidly. The plates would be adjusted till both projections were aligned on exactly the same part of the screen. Then, as the light beam switched back and forth, all the stars showed up motionless.

If one of those "stars" on the screen were a planet, however, it would have moved during the time between which the two plates were taken, and it would jump back and forth with the rapid switch between plates. If the move was a large one, the object was probably an asteroid, which would be a comparatively close object. In order for it to be a far distant planet, it would have to blink back and forth only a small amount.

The blink comparator was a great invention, because it was far easier to look at a photographic plate and watch for a single blink among many thousands of stationary stars, than to inspect each star with a magnifying glass and try to detect a small movement with the human eye alone.

Yet, even with the help of a blink comparator, Lowell's Planet X was not located in his lifetime.

3
The
Discovery
of Pluto

IN HIS WILL, Percival Lowell put one of his assistants, the American astronomer Vesto Melvin Slipher (1875–1969), in charge of the continuing search for Planet X, and he left a million dollars to the Lowell Observatory for the purpose.

However, Lowell's widow didn't want a million dollars to go to the observatory. Lowell had left her a good deal of money, too, but Mrs. Constance Lowell wanted more and turned to the law. This lost the observatory a great deal of money and a great deal of time. It was not until 1927 that everything was settled and the observatory's astronomers could return to the search.

Once that was done, the observatory found it needed a new and better telescope, and that cost more money than it now had. Fortunately, Lowell's brother also had money. He paid for a new telescope, which was put in place in 1929.

What was needed next was someone who would take photographs of the sky and use the blink comparator to look for Planet X. It would be a long and difficult job, and none of the important astronomers at the Lowell Observatory wanted to do it. Each had specialized knowledge and training and important tasks to perform. What was needed for the search was someone with very little training but with enthusiasm, patience, and a good eye.

The right man for the job turned out to be Clyde William Tombaugh (b. 1906). He was from a farm family in Illinois and, being too poor to afford college, had only a high school education. However, he was fascinated by astronomy and had worked eagerly with three telescopes he had built using parts from old machinery he found at his father's farm.

In 1928, Tombaugh wrote a letter to the Lowell Observatory, sending drawings and notes he had made of his telescopic observations. Slipher found them excellent. It didn't bother him that Tombaugh did not have advanced astronomical training. He would just be needed to stare at the blink comparator.

Tombaugh arrived at the observatory in 1929. When he found out what they wanted him to do, he was perfectly willing. He started on the project and discovered that he was entirely on his own. Others had promised to help him, but were actually too busy to do so.

Tombaugh, therefore, worked out his own improve-

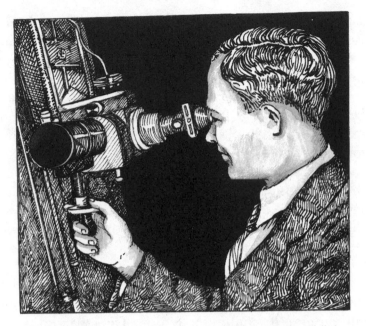

Clyde Tombaugh, the discoverer of Pluto, at the "blink comparator," an instrument used to compare photographs of sections of the sky. Tombaugh found Pluto after comparing the positions of hundreds of thousands of heavenly bodies.

ments of the blink comparator and went about the entire job himself. It was not easy. The average photographic section contained 160,000 stars, and there were some regions of the sky where he expected to have over a million stars on one plate. He found lots of asteroids that shifted position a great deal, but he didn't want them. He wanted a tiny shift that a very distant planet would make. The months passed, but that little shift didn't show up.

This seemingly futile search wasn't the only thing that discouraged Tombaugh. It didn't help that visiting astronomers were impressed by the rest of the observatory but found Tombaugh good only for a laugh. They all told him that he couldn't possibly find anything.

But Tombaugh kept grimly at his work, and on February 18, 1930, he found the blink he had been looking for. A dim "star" had moved slightly in photographs taken six days apart.

For forty-five minutes, Tombaugh kept staring at the photographic plates, unable to believe what he saw. Then he called Lampland, who carefully studied the images, and after that Tombaugh called in Slipher. Both Lampland and Slipher agreed that Tombaugh had found Planet X.

The three of them didn't rush to announce the discovery, however. They wanted to follow the planet and observe its continued motion. They wanted to be *sure*. Then, too, they wanted to announce the discovery on March 13, Percival Lowell's birthday. It would have been his seventy-fifth birthday if he had not died fourteen years earlier. They announced the discovery of the new planet on that day.

What was the new planet to be called? For a while, after the discovery of Uranus, some had wanted to call that planet "Herschel," after its discoverer. In the same way, there had been a movement to call Neptune "Leverrier," after *its* discoverer. Neither name had stuck, and astronomers eventually turned to ancient mythology in each case.

Not learning from this, Mrs. Lowell suggested the new planet be called "Percival," after her husband, or even "Constance," after herself, but such suggestions

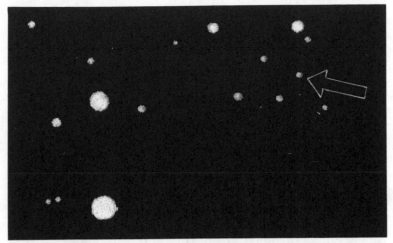

January 23, 1930

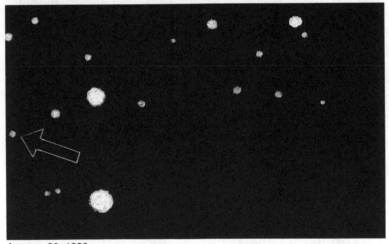

January 29, 1930

Tombaugh made his momentous discovery of Pluto when he "blinked" two photographs showing sections of the sky that looked like those shown here. The one object in a different place is Pluto. Imagine comparing photographic plates containing the images of hundreds of thousands of stars!

were dismissed at once. Slipher insisted on mythology, and he wanted "Minerva."

However, an eleven-year-old British girl named Venetia Burney suggested "Pluto." This was appropriate. For one thing, Pluto was the god of the dark underworld in the Greek myths, and the new planet swung out so far from the Sun that it could be considered to be out in a kind of dark underworld itself. For another thing, and perhaps more important, the first two letters of the name—PL—were Percival Lowell's initials. So Pluto it was.

With time, the exact orbit of Pluto was worked out. Its average distance from the Sun was about 3,672 million miles, less than either Lowell or Pickering had predicted. Pluto went around the Sun in about 248 years, again less than either's predictions. On the whole, though, Pluto's actual orbit was closer to Lowell's calculations than to Pickering's, and Pluto's position in the sky in 1930 (when it was discovered) was much closer to Lowell's predicted position than to Pickering's.

One American astronomer, Milton La Salle Humason (1891–1972), had, by the way, tried to find the distant planet using Pickering's estimate of it and its position. He did not succeed. Nevertheless, once Pluto was discovered, Humason realized he had taken photographs of the region where it was located. So why hadn't he recognized the new planet?

Humason went back to those photographs and found that two of his plates did indeed include Pluto. But one time a nearby star, brighter than the planet, had drowned it out. And the second tme, its image had

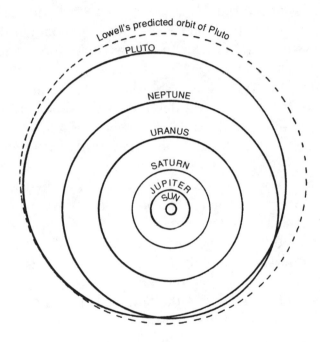

The actual orbit of Pluto differed somewhat from the orbit
predicted by Lowell

just happened to fall on a tiny flaw in the plate, so that it again didn't show.

Pluto's orbit was surprising in some ways. Until the discovery of Pluto, the solar system was flat, at least as far as the planet's motions were concerned. All the known planets orbited the Sun in very nearly the same plane. If you were to make an exact tiny model of the solar system, say, a foot across, the whole thing would fit into a flat pizza box.

Pluto, however, has an orbit that's a bit different. It is tilted about seventeen degrees to the other orbits, so that at one end it would move above the top of the pizza box and at the other end it would move below it.

What's more, Pluto's orbit is more elongated than that of the other planets. The other planets have orbits that are nearly perfect circles, but Pluto's instead is quite elliptical. At one end it is about 4,600 million miles from the Sun, but at the other end it is only 2,700 million miles from the Sun.

When Pluto is nearest the Sun—when it is at *perihelion* (PEHR-ih-HEE-lee-on, from Greek words meaning "near the Sun")—it is actually a little closer to the Sun than Neptune ever gets, up to 60 million miles closer.

If you draw the orbits of Neptune and Pluto on a piece of paper, Pluto's orbit seems to cross Neptune's at one end. It is not a real crossing, however, and there is no danger of Pluto and Neptune ever colliding. Because Pluto's orbit is tilted, the point at which the orbits cross is when Pluto is far below Neptune.

The orbit of Pluto is tilted, relative to the orbits of the other planets, and is more elongated as well.

The two planets never get closer to each other than about 1,550 million miles.

When Pluto was discovered, it was moving toward its perihelion. In 1979, it reached the point where it was as far from the Sun as Neptune was, and after that it moved slightly closer. It stays slightly closer for twenty years altogether. In 1990, Pluto is at perihelion and is as close to the Sun as it ever gets.

By 1999, Pluto will be farther from the Sun than Neptune is, and it will stay farther than Neptune for the next 229 years.

4
The Size
of Pluto

THE DISCOVERY OF Pluto produced a problem almost
at once. Lowell had reasoned that the planet he was
looking for would have to be fairly large if it were to
have enough gravitational pull to produce even a tiny
effect on Uranus's motion.

He had supposed, therefore, that the new planet
would be similar to Jupiter, Saturn, Uranus, and Neptune. Of course, the farther out one goes from the
Sun, the smaller these large planets tend to be. Jupiter
is a true giant, having a mass 318 times that of Earth,
while Saturn is smaller, with a mass only 95 times that
of the Earth's. As for Uranus and Neptune, they are
only 14.5 and 17.2 times the mass of Earth, respec-

tively. The new planet, Lowell had estimated, might have a mass 6.6 times that of Earth, and if it were as large as 10 times the mass of the Earth, even that would not be surprising. The mass should, in other words, be somewhere between one-third and one-half the mass of Neptune.

Now, Neptune has a magnitude of 7.8. If it were farther out and if its average distance from the Sun were that of Pluto, then naturally it would be dimmer and would have a magnitude of about 9. If Pluto were only one-third or one-half the mass of Neptune, it might have a magnitude of 10 or 11.

As soon as Pluto was discovered, however, astronomers determined that it had a magnitude of 15. The planet was only one-fortieth as bright as it was expected to be in Lowell's estimate. That, in fact, was one of the reasons it had been so difficult to locate.

There were three possible reasons for this surprising dimness:

1. Perhaps Pluto was considerably more distant than expected.
2. Perhaps Pluto was made of darker materials than expected.
3. Perhaps Pluto was smaller than expected.

Of course, it could also be some combination of these three possibilities.

The first possibility could be eliminated at once. The distance of Pluto could be determined by the speed with which it moved around the Sun, and this could be determined from the speed with which it drifted from one place in the sky to another. There was no question about its speed and therefore no question about its distance. And since Pluto was a bit closer to the Sun than Lowell had suggested, it should have been brighter than expected, not dimmer.

Could Pluto be made of a dark material that reflected little light? The giant planets—Jupiter, Saturn, Uranus, and Neptune—all have thick, deep, cloud-topped atmospheres. The clouds reflect about half the light that falls upon them. If Pluto were more massive than Earth, it should also have a cloudy atmosphere that would reflect half the light it receives. It can't be large *and* dark at the same time.

That leaves us with the third possibility—that Pluto is considerably smaller than Lowell had expected. It could be no larger than Earth, and might have only a thin atmosphere that reflected little light. That was the only way of accounting for its dimness.

If Pluto were an Earth-like body, its solid surface might be seen and that surface might be lighter in some places and darker in others. If the planet rotated, light parts and dark parts would alternate and the light would seem to flicker in a regular way.

In 1954, the Canadian astronomer Robert H. Hardie and a colleague, Merle Walker, measured the brightness very precisely and did indeed find that it varied regularly. From the rate of variation, they determined that Pluto rotates once every 6.4 Earth days.

But just how large is Pluto?

One way of determining its size is to look at it through a telescope strong enough to magnify it into a little globe. The width of the little globe could be measured. Knowing the magnification of the image and the distance of Pluto, the diameter could be worked out.

Diameters of globes are determined by *angular measure*. The complete circuit of the sky is divided into 360 degrees. Each degree is divided into 60 minutes of arc, and each minute of arc is further divided into 60 seconds of arc. Thus, the Sun has a diameter of about 32 minutes of arc, or just over half a degree. This means that if you imagine 675 circles, each the size of the Sun, and put them side by side they would stretch completely around the sky.

The planet Venus, when it is closest to the Earth, is about 1 minute of arc in diameter. This means that 32 dots the size of Venus, side by side, would stretch across the apparent width of the Sun. Distant Neptune is 2.2 seconds of arc in diameter, so that 27 dots the size of Neptune would stretch across the apparent width of Venus.

Pluto is nearest to us at its perihelion. If it were the size of Earth, then at perihelion it would have a width of 0.57 seconds of arc, or about one-fourth the apparent width of Neptune.

Now, all we have to do is magnify Pluto into a little globe and see what its apparent width really is.

The job was tackled by the Dutch-American astronomer Gerard Peter Kuiper (KOY-per, 1905–1973). Kuiper had specialized in the distant reaches of the solar system. He was the first to show that Saturn's largest satellite, Titan, had an atmosphere. In 1948, he discovered a fifth satellite of Uranus, which he

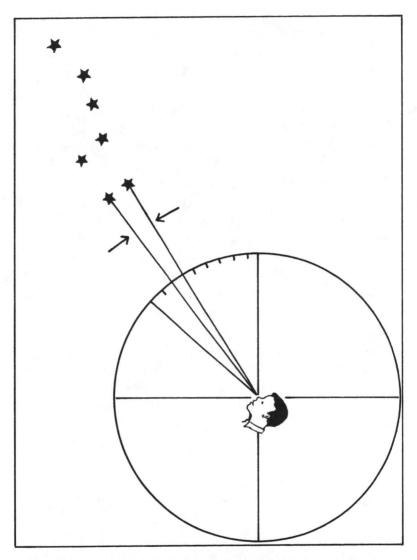

The system of angular measure divides the sky into 360 degrees, each degree into 60 minutes of arc, and each minute of arc into 60 seconds of arc. The size of a heavenly body can be measured using this system. In 1950, Gerard Kuiper determined that Pluto had a diameter of 0.23 second of arc, or about 3,800 miles.

named Miranda, and in 1949 he discovered a second satellite of Neptune, which he named Nereid.

In 1950, Kuiper made use of the new 200-inch telescope at Palomar, the best one then in existence, and finally managed to see Pluto as a tiny globe. Even so, Pluto was difficult to see sharply, since it appeared so tiny that it twinkled a bit. Twinkling is caused when temperature differences in the Earth's atmosphere bend the light slightly this way and that. The twinkling made the globe fuzzy and hard to measure.

Kuiper did his best, however, and allowing for the magnification produced by the telescope, he concluded that Pluto had a width of 0.23 seconds of arc, less than half of what would have been expected if it were the size of Earth. Kuiper therefore decided that Pluto must have a diameter of not more than 3,800 miles and that it was a bit smaller than the planet Mars.

A better way of determining the true diameter was needed, though, one that would avoid the problem of twinkling.

Every once in a while, Pluto, as it moves slowly across the sky, passes near a dim star. If Pluto happens to move directly in front of the star (an *occultation*), the star will wink out for a period of time. This is not affected by twinkling, since both Pluto and the star would be in the same place and would therefore twinkle in time with each other.

The time of occultation depends on two things: First, how fast Pluto is moving, that is, whether it covers the star with just a narrow part of itself toward one end or with its full width. Second, and most

Before calculating the diameter of Pluto, Kuiper made observations using the 200-inch Hale telescope at the Mount Palomar Observatory in Southern California.

important, how long the occultation lasts depends on just how wide the planet is.

Astronomers know how fast Pluto moves, so if the center of Pluto is located and the position of the star is measured, they can then draw a line through the part of Pluto that covers the star. From the time of occultation they can then calculate the length of that line, and from that they can calculate the width of Pluto.

On April 28, 1965, Pluto was moving toward a dim star in the constellation of Leo. If Pluto were as large as Earth, or even as large as Mars, it would have occulted the star with some part of itself. Instead, it *missed*. That meant it didn't stretch far enough from its own center to reach the star and wasn't even as large as Mars. Pluto had to have a diameter of less than 3,600 miles.

5
Charon

THE PROBLEM OF Pluto's actual size was finally solved, quite unexpectedly, in June 1978, by an American astronomer, James Christy.

He was studying excellent photographs of Pluto taken by a 61-inch telescope at the Naval Observatory in Flagstaff, Arizona. They were taken at high altitudes so that the twinkling produced by our own atmosphere was much reduced.

Christy studied the photographs under strong magnification, and it seemed to him that there was a bump on Pluto. Could it be that the telescope had moved very slightly while the photograph was being taken? No, for in that case all the stars in the field would have appeared as short lines, and these were all perfect points.

Christy looked at other photographs under magnification, and they all had the bump. What's more, Christy noticed that the bump wasn't in the same place from picture to picture. In great excitement, Christy got still earlier photographs of Pluto, some as much as eight years old, and from these it became clear that the bump was moving around Pluto within a period of 6.4 days, Pluto's rotational period.

Either there was a huge mountain on Pluto, or else Pluto had a nearby satellite. Christy was sure it was a satellite, and this was proved in 1980, when the French astronomer Antoine Labeyrie, working on top of Mauna Kea in Hawaii, made use of a technique called "speckle interferometry." This technique showed Pluto as a pattern of dots, but it produced two patterns, a larger and a smaller, with no connection between them. Pluto definitely had a satellite.

Christy named the satellite Charon (Kair-ron) after the name of the ferryboat pilot who, in the ancient myths, carried the souls of the dead across the River Styx into Pluto's underground kingdom of Hades. The name Persephone (pur-SEF-oh-nee), who was Pluto's wife in the myths, might have been better, but Christy was influenced by the fact that his own wife's name was Charlene, and he wanted the first four letters of his wife's name to be also in the name of the satellite.

In 1980, Pluto passed close to another star. Pluto missed the star as seen from Earth, but Charon passed in front of the star, and this occultation was viewed

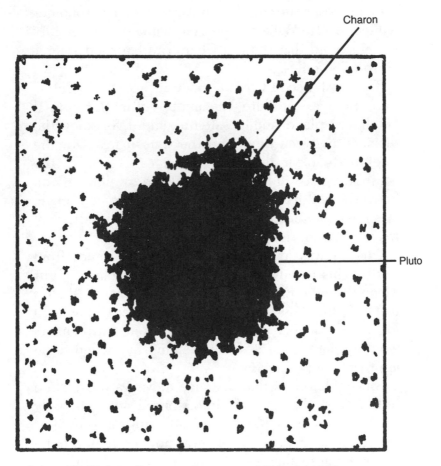

Charon

Pluto

James W. Christy discovered a moon of Pluto in 1978, seen here as a bump at the top of the drawing of Pluto. The discovery of the moon—named Charon—enabled him to fairly accurately calculate the mass of Pluto.

from an observatory in South Africa by an astronomer named A. R. Walker. The star winked out for fifty seconds, and that showed Charon to have a diameter of over 730 miles.

The existence of Charon made it possible to determine the mass of Pluto, the amount of matter in it. If you have a planet and its satellite, and if you know the distance between them and the time it takes for the satellite to orbit the planet, you can calculate the combined mass of the planet and the satellite. If you know the width of each and suppose that each is made of similar materials, you can calculate the individual masses of both the planet and the satellite.

Charon was found to be only 12,205 miles from Pluto. This is only one-twentieth the distance of our Moon from the Earth, so it's no wonder that, at Pluto's distance from us, a satellite so near went unnoticed for nearly half a century. Even then astronomers wouldn't have seen it if Pluto hadn't happened to be approaching perihelion.

Since Charon at that distance moved around Pluto in 6.4 days, the mass of Pluto worked out to be only 1/455 the mass of Earth, and not quite one-sixth as massive as our Moon. There was now no reason to be surprised at its dimness. It was a very small world.

Now even if we know Pluto's mass, that still doesn't tell us how large its diameter is. That would depend partly on what kind of material it was made of. A wooden ball, for instance, would be considerably larger than an iron ball of the same mass, because iron is denser than wood.

Fortunately, astronomers had another stroke of

luck. Charon revolves about Pluto in such a way that for five years near its perihelion we see it pass from north to south in front of Pluto and then pass from south to north behind Pluto. Charon started this series of eclipses in 1985, just seven years after its discovery, and the eclipses came to an end in 1990. If Charon had been discovered twelve years later, astronomers would have missed the eclipses entirely.

These eclipses have been important, since from them astronomers have been able to calculate the diameter of Pluto from the time it takes Charon to pass in front of Pluto, or from the time Charon remains hidden behind it. It is just like the occultation of a star taking place every 6.4 days.

It turns out that Pluto is 1430 miles across, only about two-thirds the diameter of our Moon. This is smaller than anyone had thought. Charon is 740 miles across, a little over half as wide as Pluto. Charon's mass is about one-seventh that of Pluto.

The Pluto–Charon combination is particularly interesting for two reasons. First, when a small world circles a large one, the rotation of the small world is slowed by the tides set up in it by the gravitational pull of the large one. This slowing continues until eventually the small world faces the same side to the large one at all times. Thus, our Moon faces only one side to Earth.

In the same way, Charon faces one side to Pluto at all times, but Pluto is so small that its rotation has also been slowed, and it faces only one side to Charon. As Charon rotates about Pluto and as Pluto turns on its

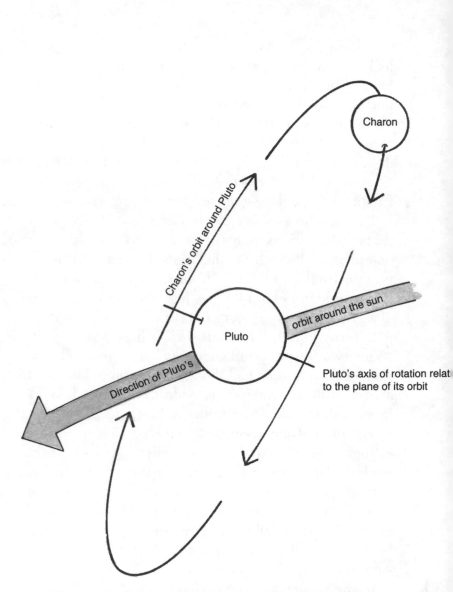

Charon

Charon's orbit around Pluto

orbit around the sun

Pluto

Direction of Pluto's

Pluto's axis of rotation relat
to the plane of its orbit

The relationship between the orbits of Charon around Pluto
and of Pluto around the Sun. When Pluto is closest to the
Sun, as it was from 1985 to 1990, viewers on Earth can
observe Charon, eclipsing Pluto.

axis, the two keep right in step. It is the only case of this sort we know of in our solar system.

Second, there is the issue of Charon's mass. Generally, satellites are very small compared with the planet they circle. Before Charon was discovered, the largest satellite in terms of its planet's mass was our own Moon. Our Moon is about one-eightieth the mass of the Earth, and no other known satellite is anywhere near that fraction of the mass of its planet. Indeed, some astronomers thought of the Earth and the Moon as a double planet—until Charon was discovered.

Since Charon has one-seventh the mass of Pluto, the Pluto–Charon combination is much more nearly a double planet than is the Earth–Moon combination.

During the eclipses, astronomers have had a chance to learn more about Pluto and Charon by studying the light they reflect. When Charon is behind Pluto, we see only the reflected light of Pluto. When Charon comes out from behind Pluto, we see the reflected light of both. If we subtract the reflection of Pluto, we are left with the reflected light of Charon only.

From this reflected light, astronomers decided by 1987 that the surface of Pluto was rich in methane, a substance which on Earth is a major part of the natural gas we use as fuel. Methane freezes at a very low temperature, so that even in Pluto's unbelievable cold, some of it would still be a gas. Pluto has a methane atmosphere about 1/900 as dense as Earth's and one-tenth as dense as that of Mars. Pluto seems to be lighter at its poles, where more of the methane freezes than at its equator.

Pluto's surface is slick with ice-like solid methane,

An artist's conception of Charon viewed from the
frozen-methane surface of Pluto.

so it reflects more light than most small worlds close to the Sun do. If it were a rocky world, it would reflect considerably less light and would be even dimmer than it is. It would have been much harder to discover.

Charon's reflected light is quite different from Pluto's. Because Charon is smaller than Pluto, it has a smaller gravitational pull. It can't hold on to the molecules of gaseous methane very well, so that any it may have once had escaped long, long ago. What is left is frozen water, which doesn't vaporize at Charon's frigid temperatures and therefore isn't lost.

Consequently, where Pluto has mostly a frozen-methane surface, Charon has a frozen-water surface. Charon has no atmosphere of its own, but Pluto's methane atmosphere seems to stretch out so far from the little planet that its very thin outermost fringe of atmospheric gas extends beyond Charon. Charon thus circles Pluto inside wisps of Pluto's atmosphere.

6
Beyond
Pluto

ONCE PLUTO WAS discovered, astronomers concluded from its dimness that its discovery was just a lucky coincidence. Pluto was clearly too small for its tiny gravitational pull to have any noticeable effect on Uranus.

Pluto was found almost exactly where Lowell had said the distant planet would be, but Pluto was not the object Lowell was looking for. It just happened to be in the right spot.

Well, then, if the tiny errors in Uranus's motion were to be explained, there must be still another planet, a tenth planet, which must lie beyond Pluto. It would be larger than Pluto in order to produce the effect on Uranus, and the farther beyond Pluto it was, the larger it would have to be.

On the whole, then, even if it were farther than Pluto, its larger size would make it brighter than dim little Pluto, and therefore it would be easier to find.

But where is it?

Tombaugh, who had discovered Pluto and then realized it couldn't be Lowell's Planet X, exactly, continued to use his blink comparator for years afterward, and by 1943 he had examined 45 million stars. In the process, he found all sorts of astronomical objects far outside the solar system. Inside the solar system, he discovered a new comet and no fewer than 775 asteroids that hadn't been seen before. But he found no new planet.

If there were a tenth planet the size of Neptune, Tombaugh could have spotted it even if it were 43,600 million miles away, or twelve times as far away as Pluto's average distance from the Sun. Even if it were only a third the size of Neptune and far beyond Pluto, he could have spotted it.

After fourteen years of searching, however, Tombaugh concluded rather wearily that there were no new planets to be found within 5,500 million miles of the Sun, and that if planets existed beyond that, they would be too far away to have much influence on the orbits of Uranus or Neptune.

Yet not all astronomers are satisfied with that conclusion. After all, it is possible to see a planet and yet not recognize it. Think of Humason taking two photographs of Pluto and missing both times because of the interference of nearby stars and of flaws on the photographic plate.

Besides, if there is no planet out there, then what is causing the small error in Uranus's motion? What's more, Neptune has now moved far enough around its long orbit that errors in its motion have also been detected and *something* must be causing it.

An astronomer named Conley Powell has recalculated the errors of the planet Uranus. He felt that since 1910, much better observations had been made of Uranus than before, and that perhaps only those observations made after 1910 ought to be considered. He worked out the error since then and calculated that there might be a tenth planet with three times the mass of Earth, and at a distance of 5,650 million miles from the Sun. It would circle the Sun every 494 years. Powell even predicted where in the sky it should be found.

In 1987, Powell persuaded astronomers at Lowell Observatory to search for the planet at the indicated spot. They did, but found nothing.

Of course, even if the planet exists, its orbit may be so eccentric that it is not likely to be found. The orbit might be greatly tipped with respect to the other planetary orbits, and it may be extremely lopsided. Perhaps only when it approaches its perihelion does it affect the outer planets. It may have reached perihelion during the last couple of centuries and done its work to help us find Neptune and Pluto. But it may now be on its way far out where it can't be seen, and it may not return to perihelion for eight centuries or so.

There are now more sophisticated telescopes, and there are rockets and probes that venture far out into space. Someday these might spot something. It is also possible that we might study cometary orbits that reach out beyond Neptune and Pluto and see if any errors are found in their orbits that could be blamed on a tenth planet. Some rocket probes have now passed beyond Neptune and Pluto and some errors in their motions might be blamed on a tenth planet. However, so far *nothing* has showed up that has been any help at all.

Yet something unexpected may turn up (like Charon, or Pluto itself) when astronomers are expecting nothing, or when they have given up all hope. It's just that the unexpected may not turn up for many years.

Or, you know, it could turn up tomorrow.

Index